AF390338

R.E.I. Editions

All of our ebooks can be read on the following devices:
- Computers
- eReaders
- iOS
- Android
- Blackberries
- Windows
- Tablet
- Cell phone

French Academy

Sahasrara

The Seventh Chakra

ISBN: 978-2-37297-4813

Publication: January 2013
Copyright © 2013 R.E.I. Editions
www.rei-editions.com

Work plan

1- Muladhara - The First Chakra

2 - Svadhishtana - The Second Chakra

3 - Manipura - The Third Chakra

4 - Anahata - The Fourth Chakra

5 - Vishuddha - The Fifth Chakra

6 - Ajna - The Sixth Chakra

7 - Sahasrara - The Seventh Chakra

French Academy

Sahasrara
The Seventh Chakra

R.E.I. Editions

Book Index

The chakra system 11

Sahasrara - Tha Seventh Chakra 15

How to activate the 7th chakra 24

Color of the seventh chakra 25

Essential oils associated with the seventh chakra 29

    Laurel 30

    Incense 34

    Geranium 40

    Rose 45

    Vetiver 50

Himalayan flowers for the seventh chakra 55

    Flight 57

Californian flowers for the seventh chakra 58

    Angel's Trumpet 60

    Angelica 62

    Fawn Lily 64

Lotus 65

Purple Monkeyflower 66

Australian flowers for the seventh chakra 68

Bush irises 70

Bach flowers for the seventh chakra 72

Water violet 74

Impatiens 76

Heater 79

Chicory 82

Agrimony 84

Walnut 86

Rescue Remedy 88

Number of the seventh chakra 92

Phisical exercises 96

Stones for the 7th Chakra 98

Hyaline Quartz 100

Rainbow Obsidian 102

Diamond 104

Moonstone 106

White onyx 109

Rutilated Quartz.................................... 110

Selenite.. 112

Celestine 114

The chakra system

The word Chakra, which comes from Sanskrit and means "wheel", is meant to indicate the seven basic energy centers in the human body. Chakras are centers of subtle psychic energy located along the spine. Each of these centers is connected, at the level of subtle energies, to the main ganglia of the nerves which branch off from the vertebral column. In addition, the chakras are related to the levels of consciousness, to the archetypal elements, to the phases inherent in the development of life, to the colors, which are closely linked to the chakras, because they are found outside our body, but inside the aura , or the electromagnetic field that surrounds each person, to sounds, body functions and much, much more. The Eastern doctrine that has spread knowledge of them in the Western world considers the Chakras as openings, gateways to the essence of the human body. The chakras are usually represented inside a lotus flower, with a variable number of open petals. The open petals represent the chakra in its full opening. On each petal is written one of the fifty letters of the Sanskrit alphabet, which are considered sacred letters, therefore, divine expression. Furthermore, each of them expresses a different activity of the human being, a different state, both manifest and still potential. Each chakra resonates on a different frequency which corresponds to the colors of the rainbow.

The seven main Chakras also correspond to the seven main glands of our endocrine system. Their main function is to absorb the Universal Energy, metabolize it, break it down and convey it along the energy channels up to the nervous system, feed the auras and release energy outside. Most everyone sees them as funnels, simultaneously swirling and flowing energy back and forth. Each of the seven centers has both an anterior (usually dominant) component and a posterior (usually less dominant) component, which are intimately connected, with the exception, however, of the first and seventh, which, however, are single.

From the second to the fifth, the anterior aspect relates to feelings and emotions, while the posterior aspect relates to the will. As regards the anterior and posterior sixth, and the seventh, the correlation is with the mind and reason. The first and seventh. they also have the very important connection function for the human being: being the most external Chakras of the energy channel, they have the characteristic of placing man in relation with the Universe on one side and with the Earth on the other. The perfect functioning of the energy system is synonymous with good health. There are many techniques to open the Chakras, including Reiki, which stands out for its peculiar sweetness and for the possibility of harmonizing any energy imbalances.

Each center oversees certain organs, and has particular functions on an emotional, psychic and spiritual level. Among the seven fundamental ones, there are precise affinities.

- The First with the Seventh: Basic Energy with Spirit Energy.
- The Second with the Sixth: Energy of feeling on a material level with Energy of feeling on an extrasensory level.
- The Third with the Fifth: Energy of the working mind and personal power with Energy of the higher mind and communication.
- The Fourth: bridge between the upper three and the lower three and alchemical forge of transformation.

Each Chakra is associated with a color, which corresponds to and derives from the frequency and vibration of the center itself. Furthermore, each Chakra corresponds to a mantra, the sound of a musical note and, in some cases, even a natural element, a planet or a zodiac sign. Because the chakra system is the primary processing center for every function of our being, blockage or energetic insufficiency in the chakras usually causes unrest in body, mind, or spirit. A defect in the flow of energy through a given chakra will cause a defect in the energy supplied to the connected parts of the physical body, as well as affect all levels of being. This is because an energy field is a Holistic entity; every part of it affects every other part. Essential oils are able to tune into specific chakras: their scent and their vibration gently put us in deep contact with our energy centers.

The massage with specific essential oils on the points corresponding to the chakras activates and balances their action, harmonizing and strengthening the entire body. Starting from the bottom they are:

- 1st = Muladhara
- 2nd = Swadhisthana
- 3rd = Manipura
- 4th = Anahata
- 5th = Vhishuddhi
- 6th = Ajna
- 7th = Sahasrara

Furthermore, each of the seven chakras comes to represent an important area of human psychic health, which we can briefly summarize as:

1. Survival
2. Sexuality
3. Strength
4. Love
5. Communication
6. Intuition
7. Cognition.

Metaphorically the chakras are related to the following archetypal elements:

1. Earth
2. Water
3. Fire
4. Air
5. Sound
6. Light
7. Thought

Sahasrara - Tha Seventh Chakra

The seventh chakra is the crown chakra, the vertex center.

Its color is purple, gold, white.

Its symbol is the lotus with a thousand petals, where one thousand is the result of 50 x 20: the fifty phonemes of the Sanskrit alphabet repeated twenty times, and it is located at the top of the skull, in the Bregma area.

It is a non-physical Chakra, which can essentially be defined as the interface between the individual consciousness and the cosmic, universal one.

It is here, in this chakra, that the adept experiences union with the divine, liberation, samadhi.

There is no blocked seventh Chakra, it can only be more or less developed, in relation to the individual's personal spiritual path. There are no known and specific pathologies related to this energy center, neither on a physical nor on a mental or spiritual level; we only know that the energy elaborated at this level has effects on all the tissues and functions of the organism, in a more or less evident, intense and effective way.

- The crown chakra controls the cerebrum, crown, entire brain and nervous system. It is also said to control the right eye. In Egyptian mythology, the opened Third Eye is called the Eye of Horus. The physical left eye controls the Moon and the manifested and feminine worlds and the right eye controls the unmanifested, masculine and spiritual worlds.

Thus, the Right Eye of Horus descends Spirit into matter and then feeds that Spirit into the Left Eye of Horus. In this way, the Third Eye remains open, grounded in the physical world and fully receptive.

It is the chakra that connects with one's most spiritual part, and with cosmic reality. Reaching the opening and awareness of this chakra leads to the completeness of being only if it is reached through the opening and awareness of all the other chakras, without exception. On the other hand, the disharmony of the seventh chakra leads to a closure and a lack of understanding of the spiritual part, both one's own and that of others, with, as a consequence, a decidedly materialistic vision of existence. The seventh chakra is the Light of knowledge and awareness, it is a global vision of the Universe and in everyone's growth path it can lead to the spiritual serenity of complete, universal knowledge. The seventh chakra is what brings the human being closest to total contact with his own interiority and, therefore, with the divine. It's the chakra that pushes the most aware people to try to elevate their self and connect with the Whole. Meeting a human being with the seventh chakra completely open means meeting someone absolutely out of the ordinary: a true Master.

- Only Jesus, Buddha, Osho, Mahavira, Krishna are recognized as Masters who have reached enlightenment, a level of spirituality so high that they do not need to speak.

It is enough to look at them to follow them unconditionally. The seventh chakra is located in the pineal gland and is made up of the meeting of the six chakras. It would be a hollow space, on the edges of which there would be a thousand nerves.

These nerves could be seen by sectioning the brain cross-sectionally. Prior to self-realization, this center is closed by the ego and superego. Illuminated by the awakening of the kundalini, it would become similar to a bundle of flames of seven colors which integrate eventually creating a clear crystal color flame. This would correspond to absolute freedom, joy of spirit, serenity, the relationship between the consciousness of the individual and that of the universe. This chakra would close in the event of a "near fainting" to prevent loss of consciousness and the soul from escaping. Physically it would manifest itself with vitiligo and vertigo and in the psychological field with boredom, dissatisfaction, hatred towards God. It has in its heart a smaller lotus with twelve petals in which the triangle called Kamakala is inscribed, which symbolically represents the seat of the Supreme Shakti, i.e. the unindividualized "cosmic force".

It is locat ad above the end of Sushumna; some master specifies in the middle of the brain, some others say just below the brahmarandhra, while others place it just above this. Sahasrara appears as a white lotus with luminous filaments, with "a thousand petals". Inside the full moon shines among cold silvery rays and inside it is inscribed the triangle that houses the great void, origin and dissolution of everything. Here resides Paramashiva, symbol of the identification between the individual soul and the universal soul, between man and God, realization of the supreme bliss that follows the destruction of ignorance and false vision operated by Paramashiva himself as the supreme guru who instructs the devoted yogi.

The earthly guru who led the disciple to the threshold of liberation is identified here with Paramashiva himself seated on the hamsa, the goose. The hamsa proposes the theme of unification and the overcoming of polarities to realize the ineffable Unity: the ultimate Mystery is divided into two, masculine and feminine, spirit and nature, «ham» and «sa», «I» and « this". The symbolism of reunification is further emphasized in sahasrara by the presence of the moon and sun mandalas. In the hamsa are contained all the forms that the Divine assumes and every devotee will find the one dear to his heart: for the shivaites it is Shiva, for the vishnuites it is Vishnu, for the devotees of the Goddess it is Shakti, for others it is Vishnu-Shiva.

Shakti manifests itself in sahasrara in the triangle inscribed in the mandala of the moon as Amakala, the sixteenth lunar asterism: a bright and dazzling goddess, of a solar colour, dripping a continuous trickle of ambrosia downwards. Inside Amakala, imagined as a crescent moon and therefore concave, resides Nirvanakala, also in the shape of a crescent, reddening like the sun, the heart of all beings and dispenser of divine knowledge. Inside this, in the mystical point that symbolizes the void from which everything originates and to which everything returns, we find Nirvana Shakti, dazzling like ten million suns, she before whom nothing existed: it is here that Shiva unites with Kundalini and it is from this union that the nectar of ambrosia then drips downwards.

The yogi must therefore make Kundalini ascend from the muladhara to the sahasrara, making her cross all the chakras up to lead her to her lord, Paramashiva, so that she unites with him and can enjoy the ambrosia generated by their union.

Therefore the goddess in serpentine form must be made to descend again in muladhara and, if in the ascent she had reabsorbed the elements of a chakra in the following one up to dissolving all the manifestation in the void contained in the triangle of sahasrara, now, descending again, she emanates again the chakras and all that they constitute and invest, infusing them with new life, but above all permeating them with consciousness.

Through the chakras the yogi has explored himself and the world: he has entered the mechanisms of the body to reappropriate them in a full and totally voluntary manner, he has descended beyond the threshold of the conscious into the darkness of the primitive Uroboros, the collective unconscious, to recover the his individual conscience. But he didn't stop there; he dared to go further, sacrificing his psycho-physical ego to transcend himself. So he drew on the infinite Consciousness that lies beyond the human and opened his third eye looking out onto another dimension.

An esoteric chronicle remains of this incredible journey beyond the finite, told by symbols, since only they, which cause resonances, are dynamic and transform, can express what cannot be communicated otherwise. The crowning glory of using this Chakra is therefore to connect us with the mystical and the Divine, while remaining firmly anchored to the earth and the material things it represents. In short, the maximum development of the seventh Chakra connects us to the correct balance of the first Chakra, and vice versa. After all, body energy must cyclically flow from top to bottom and vice versa.

In fact, the Indian iconography of the Chakras is also represented by two snakes spiraling around the spine, symbolizing the constant ascent and descent of energies along the body. From an emotional and character point of view, the imbalance of the seventh Chakra manifests itself with a closure in oneself, a loss of conviction in the meaning of existence, a loss of enthusiasm. In other words, it is a question of the dark side and of the difficulties relating to the positive "enlightenments" that are obtained with the liberation and nourishment of the energies of the seventh Chakra.

There is also the risk that the lack of understanding and acceptance of the changes, resulting from the spiritual awakening, determine an unpleasant rejection by the people of their lives. The crown chakra governs not only the brain's control of our entire nervous system, but also our Higher Self's control of our entire physical incarnation. Once the crown chakra is open, we can become aware of our true "brain" that exists beyond the limitations of the third and fourth dimensions.

Our ability to perceive physical life from that higher perspective allows us to gain access to our multidimensional consciousness. While in that multidimensional state, we have the ability to see the myriad forms of our existence in the many different planes and realities. The crown chakra rules Cosmic Consciousness which is our connection to spiritual wisdom, aspirations and knowledge of Truth. From this perspective, we see ourselves as a spark of consciousness that creates all and, paradoxically, "IS" all. From our Cosmic Consciousness, we are the dreamer dreaming a dream and realizing that all that is perceived is an extension of our Self.

Just as the root chakra represents our connection to the Divine Mother or Mother Earth, the crown chakra represents our relationships to the Divine Father or Sky Father.

Father Sky and Mother Earth unite, Spirit in Matter, to create the Child of Love, consciousness in physical form. Mother Earth in the first chakra roots our power and sends it upwards from the earth to unite with Father Sky in the seventh chakra. The rising of the Kundalini connects us with the energy that comes from the higher dimensions while giving us the power and responsibility, in turn, to ground that energy into the physical plane. The relationship with the mother is associated with the first chakra.

If the connection with our mother was not sufficient for our needs, we often feel cut off from our roots, from physical life and our attitudes towards home, security and money are negatively affected. Conversely, the relationship with the human father is associated with the seventh chakra. Because the crown chakra represents our oneness with life, we feel a sense of isolation from "God" and humanity if the bond with our father is insufficient.

Because the crown chakra represents our multidimensional consciousness, when we open it our reality is no longer limited to the third and fourth dimensions. When the third eye chakra, the sixth chakra opens, we begin to travel to the higher sub-planes of the fourth dimension.

With the opening of the seventh chakra, and subsequent activation of the Third Eye, consciousness can now enter the fifth dimension. It is then that the many realities around and within us gradually become apparent to us. Opening the crown chakra expands our perception into the fifth dimension where there is no polarity. Thus, there are many paradoxes associated with this chakra, as it represents the "end of all paradox".

As we journey through the higher dimensions, it is important to release all judgments associated with the polarities of light and dark. Instead, we must consult our inner awareness and higher consciousness to navigate us through our inner worlds. Eventually, we will all be aware of our fifth dimensional selves, they know no judgment and have no fear.

How to activate the 7th chakra

- Take regular walks in the mountains and, once at the top, admire the valley in complete tranquility before your eyes.
- Seek tranquillity, practice Yoga or Zen, or other techniques, as long as they lead to inner peace.
- Take more care of your spiritual development, trust your inner intuition to find suitable teachers.
- Wear white clothing or furnish your home using white or violet as much as possible, put a vase of white and/or violet flowers on the table at home.
- You can stimulate the seventh chakra by pronouncing the letter "M" for a long time. To do this, sit up with your back straight and make a long "MMMM" sound with each breath.
- Essential oils: frankincense, geranium and rose stimulate this chakra. Let a few drops evaporate in an essence diffuser or put a few drops mixed with a little milk in the bath water.
- Gemstones: The following stones strengthen the crown chakra: diamond, rock crystal, rainbow obsidian, spinel, light tourmaline, azurite. You instinctively choose a stone, then hold it in your hand letting its energy pervade your chakra, or always carry it with you set in a ring or on a necklace.

Color of the seventh chakra

The seventh chakra is associated with the color white, the color of light that includes all other colors, with violet and gold, the colors of infinity, peace and wisdom.

White by itself is not a color, as it encompasses all the others. The white color is synonymous with purity and virginity, it indicates the need for perfection. It is the color of neutrality and, therefore, can sometimes express the inability to expose oneself, to take a position. Since sunlight is only apparently white, by exposing ourselves to sunlight for about ten minutes a day, our body will have the opportunity to regenerate itself by catching the vibrations it needs from the spectrum of sunlight.

- White represents light, simplicity, sunshine, air, illumination, purity, innocence, chastity, holiness, sacredness, redemption.

White light is revitalizing, regenerates the body, clears the mind. It is the color of the new. It represents the state of bliss in which man reaches the divine state, fusion with the universal Being, the liberation of the spirit from the constraints of the body, the integration between reason and spirituality. It oversees the sense of empathy, feeling one with the Whole.

In the light spectrum, the color Purple is positioned at the antipodes of Red and symbolizes the ability to identify with others.

- Cold" type energy.

It is the ray with the greatest energetic properties of the visible spectrum. Born from the mix of red (love) and blue (wisdom) it is the color of metamorphosis, transition, mystery and magic. It is the color of spirituality but also of erotic fascination, it indicates the union of opposites, suggestibility. Purple often represents wealth and justice and passivity.
In the spectrum, purple ranks behind blue.
In nature, its various shades are mixtures of red and blue; therefore also in occult symbolism, it is to be considered in this color, the presence of red, color of Fire and of life, and that of blue, air, Heaven.
Today, as in antiquity, purple represents the transition between life and immortality.
It is spirituality veiled by a tinge of sadness or melancholy, which implies the remembrance of earthly things.

- It is excellent for deep meditation, therefore to free the mind from all activity and to obtain a better inner vision of oneself.
- Purple is the color of Neptune and Pisces, and one of the colors of Jupiter and Sagittarius.
- Its effects on the organism: stimulates the production of white blood cells, the spleen, the osteo-skeletal development.

- It also optimizes the sodium-potassium ratio and fights bladder and kidney disorders.

It is useful against sciatica and neuralgia, it is active against eczema, psoriasis, acne.

Blood purification, it slows down cardiac activity and promotes cerebral microcirculation, for this reason it is used to counteract baldness. Excellent healer. Combined with the seventh Chakra, Violet highlights and accentuates the emotional part of the individual, consequently making him fragile and easily attacked. The Crown Center or Seventh Chakra is the most important of all. It has 1000 petals and is known as Sahasrara. It is located in the limbic area of the brain. All this expresses the concretization of Union with the Divine Power.

- It is absolute freedom, the joy of the Spirit and serenity. In the pivotal point of the Seventh Chakra we find a smaller lotus with twelve petals in which the triangle called Kamakala is inscribed, which symbolically represents the Cosmic Force.

It is the Chakra that manages the contact with Divine Knowledge. The Crown Chakra is located in the pineal gland and is made up of a single pole. The wearer denotes dignity and nobility, intelligence, prudence, humility and wisdom.

The character is a bit difficult with opposite and irreconcilable tendencies.

He needs to feel free, he wants to fascinate, he arouses sympathy and admiration everywhere. He is very available and communicative, has great humanity, cultivates high-level, cultured and sensitive interests. Desires to help others in a meaningful way, has an inclination for the occult, magical and arcane. He has good taste and takes great care of his physical appearance. Refined lover of beauty and art.

Essential oils associated with the seventh chakra

Laurel, frankincense, lotus, geranium, rose and vetiver activate the seventh chakra. Mix each individual essential oil with a carrier oil, such as jojoba or almond oil, in the ratio of 2 drops per tablespoon of carrier oil, then 2 drops per 10 mL of carrier. Since this is a "vibrational treatment", a very diluted mixture will have a deeper and more marked action. Massage the chakra you want to work on with the blend containing the chosen essential oil. Use a few drops and apply them slowly with your fingertips and in a clockwise circular motion. While massaging the Chakra, focus on the result you want to achieve, visualizing the harmonic energy of the oil as it opens and rebalances the chakra. After the treatment, lie down and relax for a while, allowing the Chakra to rebalance itself. Breathe deeply and slowly, trying to clear and empty your mind as much as possible.

As an alternative to the massage, add a few drops of the essential oil chosen for the treatment to the essence diffuser. Concentrate and focus on your therapeutic intention, visualize the aromatherapy energy of the essential oil, open and rebalance the chakra. Relax for at least half an hour.

Laurel

Laurel oil is a real stimulant, it strengthens the ability to concentrate and memory and calms anxiety and fears. This is why it is very useful in case of exhaustion, tiredness and stress. It's also good for the environment: putting a drop in the essential oil burner helps eliminate insects. For the Ancients it was the tree consecrated to the Sun-Apollo, its leaves crowned the head of heroes, geniuses and sages.

The Greeks, in fact, thought that its leaves had the power to communicate the gift of divination, to ward off bad luck and contagious diseases. At Delphi, seat of the oracle of Apollo, the god's priests and the pythia chewed or burned laurel leaves to establish communication with the gods and slept on "mattresses" made of layers of its twigs, to favor premonitory dreams. In Rome it was considered the sign of triumph, so much so that the victorious generals wore a crown made with its fronds when they were celebrated on the Campidoglio. In fact, it is said that it was Jupiter himself who gave it to Caesar to celebrate the emperor's victories. This essential oil belongs to the group of heart notes and its multiple properties, antiseptic, expectorant, antirheumatic, digestive, recommend its use especially in affections of the respiratory and digestive systems.

Laurel essential oil is made up of 45% eucalyptol. It is for this reason that by diluting this essential oil in a good carrier oil, a calming effect can be obtained for muscle pain and spasms.

The extraction of laurel essential oil has a moderate yield. From 30 kg of raw material about 700 ml of hydrosol and 45 ml of essential oil are obtained.

- Part used: leaves.
- Extraction method: steam distillation.
- Heart note: herbaceous, fruity, fresh, slightly balsamic scent.

Stimulating: if inhaled, it gently activates energy, strengthens the ability to concentrate and memory; develop creativity; calms fears and exam anxiety. When you lack self-confidence, you are afraid of public speaking, fear of not being up to or of failing to achieve your goals: it promotes psychic awareness and intuition, "making the impossible possible". Useful in case of exhaustion, tiredness and stress.

- **Rebalancing**

Restores the sebaceous balance in dermatitis which is often the cause of acne and inflammation. It can be added to liquid soap, it protects the skin and has a delicate antiseptic action. Therefore excellent for those who have to wash their hands often: dentists, doctors, nurses, masseurs. It is an effective remedy to strengthen hair and prevent hair loss. If rubbed regularly and consistently on the scalp, it stimulates microcirculation, promoting oxygenation and nourishment of the tissues, counteracting alopecia. Prevents hair loss by strengthening it at the root, 2 drops of laurel and 2 drops of sweet orange in a hair lotion to tone and stimulate regrowth.

- **Digestive**

2 drops of laurel essential oil in a teaspoon of honey taken after meals helps digestion and soothes stomach pains. If diluted in vegetable oil and massaged on the stomach, it has a relaxing action on the smooth muscles of the gastrointestinal system. Useful in the presence of spasms, irritable bowel and to eliminate gases that cause meteorism and flatulence. Chewing a leaf before meals helps those with difficult digestion and fights fermentation. In case of gastric pain or dysentery it is helpful to take 1 teaspoon of honey with 1 drop of laurel essence. Let it dissolve in a glass of water and drink it slowly.

- **Environmental diffusion**

1 drop for every square meter of the environment in which it spreads, using an essential oil burner, helps to eliminate insects.

- **Massage oil**

Dilute at 4 - 6% in 100 ml of sweet almond oil and rub in in case of pain and muscle sprains.

- **Contraindications**

Laurel essential oil is contraindicated during pregnancy and should be used in moderation, because at high doses it can be narcotic or cause dermatitis. Although it also acts on the digestive system, it is advisable to take it only externally, since taken orally it can have narcotic effects.

On the other hand, under no circumstances should you take the berries, as they contain toxic substances that cause the destruction of white blood cells.

Incense

Known for its numerous properties, it is an antiseptic and antirheumatic, also useful in case of cough, cold and to rebalance the nervous system. Balsamic and expectorant, tonic of the urogenital system, antiseptic, anti-inflammatory and healing, fights skin aging, calms anxiety and fears, keeps mosquitoes away. Frankincense also has a beneficial effect on the epidermis: it is a good antiseptic, anti-inflammatory and healing agent and is particularly useful for fighting wrinkles and skin aging. The Egyptians had introduced incense in their fumigation practices and for cosmetic use: rejuvenating masks and for the preparation of kohl, a sort of kajal for eye make-up. The Jews met it during their stay along the coasts of the Red Sea and included it in their religious practices: connected to the birth of Jesus, brought to him as a gift by the Magi. Even among the Arab peoples, incense was widely used and constituted an exchange wealth. It was also called Olibanum (white). The most valuable variety is, in fact, represented by white grains.

The most precious Frankincense essential oil grows at an altitude of 700 meters and comes from Dhofar (Yemen). The tree is engraved in the bark, from which a milky liquid comes out which, in contact with the air, thickens and turns brown, orange, yellow, white, moon drops, with grains almost as large as a walnut ; the grains are selected by the women who separate the delicates from the moonlight color, these give the best quality incense.

- Part used: rubber resin.
- Extraction method: steam distillation.
  - Base note: sweet, balsamic scent. Its perfume is particularly suitable for meditation as it has the property of joining matter to the subtle world of the spirit. It is the purifier par excellence, stimulates mental activity and calms tormented feelings.

- **Aromatherapy**

It is used as a sedative to relieve nervousness, anxiety, black mood, gives courage and confidence. It can be used in the diffuser for meditations. Tonic and rebalancing of the central nervous system, calms anxious forms, stress agitations, obsessive thoughts, fears. In fact, it prepares for calm, meditation and prayer.

- Against sadness and negative moods, spread 3 or 4 drops of essential oil in the environment; alternatively, take a hot bath by diffusing 5 or 6 drops of essence into the water.
- To fully relax, it will be very useful to perform a light massage on the forehead and temples with

2-3 drops of incense essential oil diluted in 1 tablespoon of vegetable oil.

- **Antiseptic**

Purifies the air and the environment in which it is diffused. Useful in case of bacterial disorders, it carries out its antimicrobial action.
Antirheumatic: applied diluted for friction and massage, this warm and balsamic oil penetrates deeply, warms the part and re-oxygenates the tissues, taking away the pain.

- **Balsamic**

Frankincense has excellent antimicrobial and balsamic properties. Treats respiratory diseases and asthma. Free from phlegm and colds. In the presence of cough and phlegm, prepare a massage oil by diluting 20 drops of incense essential oil in 50 ml. of almond oil. Apply to the chest with a massage in the morning and evening.

- **For purifying masks**

Add 2 drops of incense essential oil to a spoonful of sweet almond oil to add to ventilated clay already diluted in water. The astringent power adds up to purify the skin of the face and neck.

- **Anti-aging cream**

Add 2-3 drops of incense essential oil in the jar of the moisturizing or firming cream that you normally use to enhance its effect.

- In case of stress wrinkles: use 1 drop of incense oil with 1 drop of Sandalwood oil and 1 drop of Jasmine oil mixed in the face cream.
- As an anti-wrinkle tonic: dilute 3 drops of incense essential oil in 10 ml of rosehip oil and apply in a light veil on the face and neck. Or dilute 5 drops each of the essential oils of frankincense, lavender, lemon, cypress and rose in 50 ml of jojoba or wheat germ oil and apply to the face 2 times a day, massaging lightly until completely absorbed.
- As an anti-wrinkle mask: dilute 5 drops of incense essential oil and 1 tablespoon of oatmeal in 2 tablespoons of natural yogurt and spread over face and neck. Rinse with warm water after about twenty minutes.
- For stretch marks: add 2 drops of incense essential oil and 2 drops of sandalwood to a hazelnut of base cream and apply to the affected part, massaging until completely absorbed. The best results are obtained in case of recent stretch marks.
- Astringent: diluted and applied to the skin, it is an excellent remedy for dilated pores and epidermal laxity.

- **Antirheumatic massage**

3 drops of incense essential oil in two tablespoons of sesame oil, to be rubbed on the part to be treated. Cover with a warm cloth and leave to absorb.

- **Fumigate**

In case of respiratory tract congestion and cough, dilute 2 drops of incense essential oil, 2 of eucalyptus and 1 of Scots pine in a bowl of boiling water and inhale.

- **Bath**

Pour 5 or 6 drops of essential oil into the bathtub, add a few drops of eucalyptus and soak for at least 10/15 minutes. In the presence of colds or flu with persistent cough, 6 drops of incense essential oil and 6 of cypress mixed in a spoonful of whole honey will be added to the hot water for the bath.

- **For local irrigation**

In case of cystitis, add 5 drops in 250 ml of boiled water, to be used daily for local applications.

- **Contraindications**

No particular contraindications have been reported, except for internal use, as for all essential oils which must be used with caution and always conveyed; for example, honey is an excellent carrier of essential oils. A curiosity instead linked to the aroma of incense: it seems that it dampens sexual desire, perhaps incompatible with its strong spiritual value.

Geranium

In aromatherapy, geranium essential oil is used in case of acne, anxiety, depression, stress, insomnia and sore throat.

Geranium essential oil has antibacterial, antidepressant, anti-inflammatory, antiseptic, astringent, diuretic, repellent and tonic properties. This makes it suitable for use on a variety of health and well-being issues. It is also used to promote emotional stability, to relieve pain thanks to its pain-relieving properties, to stimulate the healing of burns and wounds thanks to its healing properties, to improve mood and to reduce inflammation. It is useful for performing leg massages to reactivate circulation. Originally from South Africa, geranium was introduced into Europe in the 17th century by English and Dutch colonists, who, returning from the Indies, stopped with their ships at the Cape of Good Hope to get supplies.

In our continent it has begun to be cultivated, especially in the Mediterranean area, which has a climate similar to that of its origin. Geranium is made up of hundreds of different species, each characterized by its own colours, intensity of perfume, petals and degree of resistance to temperatures.

In the past it was widely used to combat bleeding thanks to its strong astringent and healing action; today it is widespread, above all as an ornamental plant and its essential oil is used by the cosmetic, food and liqueur industries.

The oil that is extracted from the geranium, as soon as it is distilled, looks like a green liquid with a very delicate sweetish smell, which is then worked and mixed according to the needs or left in its pure state.

- Part used: leaves and flowers.
- Extraction method: steam distillation
- Heart note: fresh, sweet, floral scent.

- **Rebalancing**

It is used in aromatherapy to increase imagination and intuition so as to be able to find solutions in tangled or difficult situations. It stimulates the will and desire to express yourself and to bring out what you feel deep down, it helps to become aware and balance the give-and-take. Very suitable for people who don't know what they want, it stimulates motivation in them. Attract to us all that is positive. It helps promote sleep and relaxation. You can apply a few drops on a handkerchief to place on the bedside table or keep close to the pillow, or give a neck and shoulder massage before going to sleep.

- **Astringent**

In poultices with a few drops of essence it proves to be particularly effective on areas affected by acne and pimples; in case of oily skin, in which there is a need to close the pores, to help the skin compact. In 200 ml of cold water add 8 drops of essence, with sterile gauze compresses make compresses against acne and furunculosis, taking care to change the compress when it gets hot.

- **Anti-inflammatory**

Used for gargling and rinsing, it is recommended in the treatment of congestion affecting the mucous membranes of the oral cavity, so it is useful in the presence of sore throat, pharyngitis and gingivitis.

- **Antispasmodic**

Diluted in sweet almond oil and massaged on the lower abdomen, it relaxes uterine contractions due to ovulation and menstrual pain; helps relieve the discomforts of menopause and PMS, neuralgia and headaches.

- **Invigorating**

Indicated in massages to reactivate blood circulation, to fight cellulite, and in the treatment, prevention or normalization of disorders that originate from a malfunction of the circulatory system, such as varicose veins, capillary fragility and couperose. Geranium essential oil is considered helpful in preventing and relieving wrinkles. That's why it is used as an ingredient in anti-aging creams.

You can add a single drop of geranium essential oil to the moisturizer you usually use for your face.

- **After Sun**

As after-sun, dilute 5 drops of Geranium essential oil, 5 of Chamomile and 1 of Peppermint in a spoonful of Jojoba Oil and add to the bath and/or rub before going to sleep.

- **Healing**

Diluted at 5-10% it promotes the healing of sores, cuts and burns and sunburn. To heal scars, it is recommended to mix 10 drops of geranium with 5 drops of helichrysum and 5 drops of lavender on 50 ml of jojoba oil or rosehip oil and use it regularly 2 times a day for a period of 2-3 weeks .

- **Insect repellent**

Geranium essential oil fights mosquitoes, or rather drives them away, and this is why balconies and terraces often show a vast display of planters filled with these plants.

- **Environmental diffusion**

1 drop of geranium essential oil for each square meter of the environment in which it spreads, using an essential oil burner, against mosquitoes.

- **Gargle lotion**

In a glass of water at room temperature put 6 drops of geranium essential oil, against inflammation of the mouth and for sore throat.

- **Contraindications**

Geranium essential oil is considered safe, so there are no particular precautions to follow. It's important to remember that the improper use of essential oils can be harmful, so always rely on the advice of an herbalist.

Rose

The rose, a flower with exceptional properties, is an extraordinary rebalancing agent capable of strengthening the nervous system, promoting digestion and reawakening sexuality. Spring stress, which occurs after months of work, affects the health of the body, absorbing our energies and causing a lowering of the immune system. Rose essential oil reduces anxiety attacks, the constant feeling of tension and agitation generated by stress and the consequent somatic manifestations. Known for its numerous properties, it carries out a balancing, soothing and harmonizing action, useful for self-esteem and against anxiety and wrinkles. The rose is the archetype of the flower and the symbol of both profane and divine love. Known for more than 3,000 years, ancient civilizations used it as a main ingredient in the manufacture of perfumes and cosmetics along with other essential oils. The Arabs and Berbers of Morocco have been distilling and producing rose water since the 1st century BC. C and used the infusion of its leaves for the anti-stress, tonic and antiseptic properties.

- The rose is one of the most difficult essences to distill, because it takes 4 to 5 tons of petals to obtain 1 kg of essential oil. In a drop of rose essential oil there is therefore the fragrance of about 30 roses; this low · yield unfortunately justifies the high price of its essential oil. Rose essential oil is extracted from the Rosa damascena botanical species. Given the high costs of rose essential oil, there is no shortage of already diluted solutions on the market.

The harvest begins from mid-May to mid-June, at 4 in the morning and ends at 9; after this time, in fact, it becomes too hot, so the subtle volatile parts of the rose would be partially lost.

Rose essential oil is one of those essential oils which, at room temperature, gels; otherwise, when heated, it returns to a liquid state. This also determines the evidence of the genuineness of the real rose essential oil.

- Part used: flower petals.
- Method of extraction: extraction in solvent.
- Heart note: floral, soft, delicate scent.

- **Harmonizing**

When inhaled, it opens and strengthens the heart. Rose essential oil relaxes the soul and activates the disposition for tenderness and love, as it develops patience, devotion and self-esteem. Gives joy and banishes negative thoughts, balancing negative emotions caused by anger, jealousy and stress. The scent of the essence is a wonderful psychological and physical support during pregnancy: excellent for accompanying women during childbirth and welcoming the new arrival with sweetness and love. In menopause it helps to soothe sadness and depression. In case of nervous depression, take 2 drops of rose essence twice a day.

- **Balancing of the female hormonal system**

If massaged on the stomach, it calms spasms in case of menstrual pain and stops bleeding. Indicated in disorders related to hormonal imbalances, anxiety and irritability that characterize premenstrual syndrome and menopause. To stimulate liver function, dilute 2 drops in 1 tablespoon of sweet almond oil and gently massage the liver area for a few minutes without pressing, just making a light circular rubbing to let the oil penetrate.

- **Stress reliever**

4 drops of rose essential oil diluted in a spoonful of jojoba oil and applied to the center of the forehead, under the chin and around the navel, with a circular message repeated three times: here is an excellent strategy to combat stress. To complete and amplify the relaxing effect of the message, you can drink a cup of rose tea.

- **Soothing**

Suitable for all skin types, it soothes inflamed or delicate skin. In cases of sensitive, dry or mature skin, it has an astringent, toning and anti-wrinkle action. Diluted in almond oil it is effective for preparing the skin just before childbirth and for protecting it even after, it prevents prolapses and the tendency to miscarriage. Rose oil is composed of many nutrients. Among these we can mention oleic acid, linoleic acid, lycopene and vitamin A. precisely by virtue of these substances it manages to protect the skin from aging and helps to reduce wrinkles.

- **Invigorating**

Against sexual asthenia, useful for a couple's massage or for a relaxing bath with an aphrodisiac effect; it is the oil of love and eroticism, because it enhances inner beauty and mitigates conflicts by instilling peace and happiness. Prepare a massage oil by diluting 2 drops of rose essential oil and 2 drops of jasmine in 2 tablespoons of sweet almond oil.

- **Environmental diffusion**

1 drop for every square meter of the environment in which it spreads, by means of an essential oil burner, or in radiator humidifiers.

- **Aromatherapy bath**

10 drops of rose essential oil or, for an even more relaxing effect, 3 drops each of rose, ylang-ylang and sandalwood essential oils added to the hot tub water will eliminate anxiety, tension and stress, and will promote night rest.

- **Massage oil**

In 200 ml of sweet almond oil put 20 drops of essential oil, massage the body during pregnancy or in case of stretch marks and dry skin.

- **Anti-wrinkle cream**

A few drops in a neutral cream will make it a precious anti-aging remedy.

- **Contraindications**

At the recommended doses, it has no contraindications. Not suitable for children under 3 years of age, pregnant or breastfeeding women.

Vetiver

Known for its numerous properties, it is immunostimulant and antirheumatic, also useful in case of asthenia and anemia. It is indicated in case of tiredness, exhaustion, muscular and rheumatic pains, digestive problems, amenorrhea, oily skin. The fragrance of vetiver essential oil is as energetic as it is relaxing, and has sedative, toning and aphrodisiac effects. In aromatherapy, due to its multiple properties, this essence is recommended for the treatment of the most diverse ailments.

Thanks to its sedative action, vetiver essential oil counteracts nervousness and tension, and is excellent for relaxing the body and mind with a relaxing bath or massage, as well as in the treatment of insomnia.

The simultaneous calming and energizing action makes it very effective in anxious and depressive states, and to counteract psychological tiredness. The toning activity of vetiver essential oil strengthens our body, especially the immune system, stimulates circulation and is effective in counteracting degenerative processes. It is an excellent remedy for the treatment of muscular and rheumatic pains.

The purifying properties of vetiver essential oil are expressed both systemically and locally, making it useful in the treatment of circulatory disorders and cellulite. Applied to the skin, in addition to purifying it, vetiver essential oil has antiseptic, toning and regenerating effects, which make it effective in normalizing oily skin, even in the presence of acne and seborrheic dermatitis.

Vetiver roots are an ancient remedy used in Ayurvedic tradition to relieve headaches and lower fever. In the East the roots were used to create baskets and mats and then sprinkled with water so that on days of great heat they gave off the aroma of vetiver, with insect repellent properties.

- In addition to being used alone, vetiver essential oil can be combined with other oils; it goes particularly well with the essences of lavender, yarrow, rose and sage, but also with other base notes such as patchouli and sandalwood.

Vetiver essential oil is obtained by steam distillation of the dried roots of the plant. Base note, this essence shows a certain viscosity and an amber color, and tickles the nose with its sweet and fresh exotic fragrance, with earthy, woody and slightly smoky tones, which recalls the smell of the undergrowth.

- Part used: the dried roots.
- Extraction method: steam distillation.
- Base note: bittersweet, woody, earthy scent.

- **Strengthens the immune system**

Vetiver helps to strengthen the immune system and acts as a stimulant on the circulation of the liver and pancreas, thus helping the body to purify itself. Also in this case, the essential oil should be massaged by mixing 50 drops in 50 ml of base oil, preferably calophylla. Repeat the massage on the whole body 3 times a week.

- **Cleaning**

2 drops of Vetiver essential oil in soap for daily body cleansing. Added to the shampoo, it counteracts the excess of sebum in the scalp.

- **Skin toner**

To reduce inflammation and rebalance the skin, put 2 drops of essential oil in a hydroalcoholic solution to be used after cleansing the face. For oily skin put 25 drops of Vetiver essential oil in 50ml of moisturizer. Stir for a long time to mix the two ingredients. Use this cream after cleaning your face carefully in the evening before going to bed.

- **Environmental diffusion**

Add 1 drop of vetiver essential oil per square meter of room surface to the diffuser. This will make our home pleasantly scented, giving us purified air and counteracting tension and nervousness.

- **Relaxing bath**

To eliminate anxiety and stress, dilute 15 drops of vetiver essential oil in the tub. For an even more relaxing effect, immediatcly after bathing, perform a light massage on the temples and forehead with 2 drops of vetiver essential oil diluted in 1 tablespoon of almond oil.

- **Shower**

3-4 drops on a wet sponge glove gently massage the whole body.

- **For massage**

2 drops of essential oil to be mixed with an arnica ointment to be applied to soothe joint and muscle pain. Alternatively, 3 drops of Vetiver to add to a spoonful of sesame oil to be massaged on painful areas, or on the abdomen to facilitate digestion.

- **Circulation**

An excellent remedy is foot baths. Dilute 10 drops of vetiver essential oil in hot water and keep your feet immersed for at least 15 minutes. Repeat daily for twenty days.

- **Acne**

Cold compresses are effective twice a week with 200 ml of distilled water in which we will have dissolved 10 drops of vetiver essential oil.

- **Contraindications**

To be taken externally only. The essential oil must not be used pure directly on the skin or mucous membranes, because it could cause irritation.
Contraindicated during pregnancy, lactation and in infancy.

Himalayan flowers for the seventh chakra

Himalayan Flower Enhancers directly affect the various energy levels controlled by the Chakras, removing negative feelings and stimulating positive ones. The Himalayan Flower Enhancers were identified by Tanmaya in 1990, during a stay of several months in a Himalayan valley. The term Enhancers means catalysts, because the essences are not only remedies aimed at working on negative emotions and inner states but also favor very deep processes of energy rebalancing and spiritual development to bring to light qualities buried within the person. They can be taken pure alone or diluted together with Bach flowers or other flowers. Tanmaya's first preparations involved nine combinations, seven directly connected to the plexuses, better known by the Indian name of chakra plus a general catalyst and a flower particularly suitable for children; subsequently their number multiplied with the discovery of new flowers, suitable for modulating specific emotions.

They are Flowers with a very rapid and powerful effect, unlike Bach Flowers, which are among the slowest and most delicate; this power is sometimes very useful, other times it can represent a risk of excessive action. While Bach Flowers can be considered primarily emotional remedies, i.e. aimed at rebalancing human emotions, Himalayan Flowers, thanks to the nature of the soil on which they grow, essentially address the spiritual dimension of man, stimulating the need for prayer, of meditation and connection with the divine that dwells in him.

Himalayan floral essences are liquid extracts that contain the energy of the flower to be administered generally orally, and can also be used in bath water, sprayed on the body or in the environment, or combined with oil for massage.

Flight

Flight develops uniqueness, meditation, prayer, helps to go beyond the form, towards the deepest Self, to the union of body, mind and spirit. It remedies the sense of separation, isolation, voids of meaning, feelings of insignificance. Stimulates a brightness and an inner smile that are visibly reflected on the face and throughout the person's body; at the same time it relaxes the mind and gives peace and tranquility.

The dosage of essences, pure or diluted, is two drops under the tongue several times a day. If Sahasrara is not balanced, the subject can be tempted by black magic, fall victim to superstition, tend towards isolation and lose the sense of reality. The essence enhances uniqueness, meditation, prayer, the harmonious union of mind, body and spirit. Effectively counteracts the tendency to isolation.

Californian flowers for the seventh chakra

The Californian Flowers extend the Bach Flowers.
Richard Kats and Patricia Kaminski, founders of the
FES (Flower Essence Society), together with the work
of other researchers have discovered more than 150
flowers since 1979. They work on more modern and
current specific problems which at the time Bach lived
did not they were so preponderant or they weren't
talked about like today: anorexia and bulimia, sexual
disorders, diseases deriving from environmental
pollution. It is possible to create composite essences by
combining Bach and Californian flowers, as well as
essences from other flower therapy repertoires from
other parts of the world. Californian flower remedies
are prepared in the same simple way as Bach flowers,
by placing wild flower corollas in a glass bowl filled
with spring water and leaving them to infuse in the sun
for a few hours. This liquid, very rich in vital force, is
then filtered, diluted in brandy and used for the
preparation of the so-called stock bottles (or
concentrates).
The choice of essences, as with Bach flowers, is always
personalized and in relation to the mood and emotions
you want to rebalance. Once the remedy or remedies
indicated for the personal problem have been chosen,
two drops of each are poured into a small bottle with a
30 ml dropper, filled with natural mineral water and
two teaspoons of brandy as a preservative.

The dosage is 4 drops 4 times a day, for a period of a few weeks or in any case until the symptoms improve or disappear.

Being a completely natural and non-toxic cure, they have no contraindications, do not cause side effects, can be combined without problems with both traditional and homeopathic medicines (of which they are considered complementary) or other flower therapy remedies.

Angel's Trumpet

This flower is used to entrust oneself in the great passage of life which is death. It's useful to face this moment in a serene way, without anguish, overcoming desires and attachments that keep us attached to the physical body. Transform fear of the unknown into an awareness of spiritual life. Also useful for those assisting dying people. Useful in situations where total surrender, unconditional surrender is required. The most difficult moments can be lived with serene awareness as evolutionary opportunities and not as extremely hard and terrifying trials. A key word to understand Angel's Tmumpet is trust - for situations where it no longer makes sense to struggle with death, or for the surrender of the ego, when the individual must submit totally to a process of spiritualization.

With Angel's Trumpet the individual is able to experience these processes as joyful transitions instead of frightening ordeals.

The individual realizes that death is a form of birth, when viewed from the spirit world, and is able to recognize the spirit beings who are waiting in the other world. This remedy is of great help for hospice work, warfare, natural disasters, and for all occasions when we are called upon to assist loved ones who are leaving the physical world; it is also helpful for therapists who have to guide the individual through processes of profound transformation, of "rebirth".

Angel's Trumpet facilitates the radical opening of the soul, transforming the fear of death into an awareness of the spiritual life.

For those who practice meditation and follow the spiritual path it is useful for the abandonment of desires and attachments.

Angelica

Biennial herbaceous plant of the Umbelliferae family. Stems erect, robust, hollow and can reach two meters in development. It lives in temperate climates. The leaves, glossy green, up to half a meter long, petiolate and equipped with a large clear sheath that surrounds the stem, are pinnate with a serrated edge. The slightly scented flowers are minute and always gathered in large compact and round umbels. Blooms in late summer, the inflorescences have a sweet scent.

Angelica, just like an angel, makes you feel protected and guided during changes or moments of transition and therefore infuses strength and courage. Gives the awareness of being protected and guided to those who are afraid of being abandoned to their fate. This feeling of being protected and protected is of the utmost importance for the inner life of the individual, as it gives him great strength and courage to face his work of transforming and healing the world.

- Angelica especially encourages the individual to establish a relationship with the spiritual world, transforming the too abstract perception of spiritual energies into a full sensation of the spiritual presence and spiritual beings.

This awareness is particularly developed towards that world of spiritual beings which is immediately on the border with the human world: the world of angels.

Through a lively relationship with the angelic realm, man receives protection and guidance in daily life, in moments of crisis or in the experience of passing. Useful in moments of great danger when one would like to abandon oneself to despair. He stimulates the body's internal defenses and strengthens the soul and makes it more aware of its capabilities and the true cause of problems. Also useful for those who care for the terminally ill and for pregnant women to help protect the child.

Fawn Lily

They are people who live in isolation, are prone to states of meditation, contemplation and prayer, but are too delicate and lack self-protection to face the world. They are not capable of living their spirituality in the world.

☐ People in need of Fawn Lily have highly developed spiritual energies, so much so that it is difficult for them to deal with the stresses and strains of modern society. Their souls are naturally inclined to states of contemplation, meditation and prayer, it is easier for them to be in these modes of spirituality than to be too much in the world.

However, the individual may become too mature and too developed in his spirituality.

- Fawn Lily people need to sow the great talents they have accumulated in order to evolve and progress, otherwise they become too introverted and emotionally cold, lacking the ability to draw strength and vitality from the physical world.

Fawn Lily stimulates the innate healing and teaching potentials of such individuals as the soul evolves from its cosmic virgin archetype into world mother, or world server.

Lotus

Catalyst for healing processes, opens to spirituality. It leads to concreteness those who tend too much to abstract themselves. Balance between spirituality and physicality.

The individual is predisposed to wear a crown of light and, in fact, is endowed with an imperceptible energy center called the crown chakra.

This chakra gives the individual a sense of dignity and an awareness of his royal or divine nature.

But the crown can only be worn properly by the person who has acquired true objectivity and inner humility.

Lotus is a specific remedy for crown chakra imbalances. It acts as a spiritual or harmonizing elixir, helping the individual to open up to their inner divinity.

However, an individual may overdevelop her spirituality. If the crown chakra is overdeveloped in relation to the other energy centers, especially the heart, the Lotus flower brings the spiritual forces back in the right direction and in balance. Lotus especially cures the tendency towards spiritual pride, or the delusion that the ego is "spiritually perfect or superior".

Lotus is an excellent remedy for inciting and harmonizing the higher consciousness and most importantly for integrating spirituality in a balanced way with the other energy centres.

Purple Monkeyflower

For those who are afraid of the occult or are too superstitious. It is the special flower for fears related to experiences of a spiritual or psychic nature.

- Like other Mimulus (Monkeyflower) species, Purple Monkeyflower addresses the fear felt by the individual. Purple Monkeyflower is specifically indicated for fear related to experiences of a spiritual or psychic nature. More particularly, Purple Monkeyflower is of great benefit to individuals, whose great need for safety and salvation leads them to rely on conventional socio-religious structures, even if this often does not fulfill the real need for their soul evolution.

This creates an internal conflict between spiritual impulses and external conventions or expectations.
The fear of "going astray" and following one's own path can then be accentuated by harsh and rigid religious dogmas that include threats of punishment and condemnation. Purple Monkeyflower is a powerful purifier and has the ability to debunk ideas based on cultural and religious superstition.
Purple Monkeyflower is also indicated for intense fear, hallucinations or paranoia caused by a sudden or unexpected spiritual initiation, such as in the case of drug use, ritual abuse or psychic manipulation. In such

cases the individual develops a deep fear of the spirit world, seeing it as demonic or terrifying.

The path to healing is that of courage to live one's true experience by facing spiritual phenomena in a calm and conscious way.

With this courage the individual is able to find true spiritual guidance, support and support for life on Earth.

Australian flowers for the seventh chakra

The Australian Bush Flowers are today 69 plus 19 essences created by the combination of Australian Flowers and were introduced by Ian White, Australian biologist and psychologist. They are not yet well known and used in Italy by the general public, but they are highly appreciated by flower therapists and we find Australian flowers included in many herbal and homeopathic complexes. They are among the most powerful and widely used flowers after Bach Flowers, they have a very high energy, one of the highest among floral remedies. Australian Aborigines have always used Flowers to treat discomfort or emotional imbalances, as was the case in ancient Egypt, India, Asia and South America.

The dose, for both adults and children, consists of seven drops to be taken twice a day (morning and evening) under the tongue, or in a little water. The essences should be taken for about twenty days or a month, except for particularly powerful essences.

Being a completely natural and non-toxic cure, they have no contraindications, do not cause side effects, can be combined without problems with both traditional and homeopathic medicines (of which they are considered complementary) or other flower therapy remedies. You can prepare a single remedy (whose action will then be particularly "targeted", deep and fast), or mix different remedies together; in this case it is advisable not to exceed 4 or 5 essences and, if possible, try to choose flowers with similar and synergistic properties to treat a specific problem.

Australian flowers are also very effective when applied to the skin and can be added to creams, gels, massage oils, medicated ointments or diluted in bath water. For a topical treatment, the recommended quantity is about 7 drops of each chosen remedy, to be mixed in half a cup of cream; instead, 15–20 drops of each essence should be poured into the bathtub.

The duration of treatment always depends on the individual response. A positive reaction is often obtained in about two weeks and on average two months are sufficient to rebalance numerous psychophysical problems.

Some particularly "powerful" flowers (such as, for example, Waratah) usually exert a very rapid action, even in a few days. Many times, after resolving an inner discomfort or conflict, other emotional imbalances can emerge, which will gradually be treated with the corresponding flowers.

Bush irises

They are violet colored flowers that bloom in early spring and grow in large quantities. But they are very delicate flowers, blooming for only a few hours, withering in the late afternoon and then vanishing, but seem to reappear a short time later because all the flowers are contained in the same thick and compact bract and the dead one is replaced by another bud.

Fear of death, materialism, rejection of spirituality, denial of all that is material, atheism, extremism. Spiritual perception of the individual and of reality beyond the material and physical plane. It allows the individual to access their spiritual dimension and to open the doors of their finer perceptions. It allows faith to penetrate the depths of the individual. These are people who are deeply attached to material possessions. Greedy, worldly, they generally have an atheistic conception of life. They may also have traits of intellectualism, disbelief, and excessive realism. The main emotions that live are: greed, fear, insecurity, possessiveness, frustration, dissatisfaction, blockage, lack of sensitivity and poor ability to get excited.

The main function of this flower is the development of spiritual life, the amplification of consciousness and the fight against fear of death. Increase perception.

When the individual has to develop his spiritual life because he finds pleasure only in excesses and in the satisfaction of his own needs, such as addictions, sex, food.

It is an excellent remedy in cases of terminal patients or dominated by fear of death by relieving the anguish and suffering associated with this transition.

- Must be combined with Sunshine Wattle.

Sunshine Wattle helps to accept and enjoy the beauty of the present, developing confidence for the future and restoring optimism. For those who don't remember the past as a happy time, they are still entangled in what happened to them and carry their negative experiences into the present as well. Feeling of always having to fight to earn something.

The flower gives optimism, hope.

It helps to realize how beautiful and a source of joy the present is, which becomes a pleasant premise for the future. Great remedy to take when life is temporarily difficult, it seems to be a big fight or when nothing good seems to be happening. The predominant emotions for people who need this essence are: disappointment, lack of attachment to life, fatalism, discouragement, sadness, lack of joy, recollection, non-affection, resignation, pessimism.

The lesson he must learn is to accept that life is not linear, but has its ups and downs.

We must learn to believe in the future.

Bach flowers for the seventh chakra

Bach flowers are an alternative medicine created by the British doctor Edward Bach, born on 24 September 1886 in Moseley from a Welsh family in England. He graduated in medicine in 1912 and immediately worked in the emergency room of the university hospital where he began to be noticed for the large amount of time he devoted to patients. He was immediately critical of other doctors, who studied the disease as if it were separate from the individual, without focusing on the patients themselves.

It is well known that our emotional states have a profound influence on our well-being and health. An altered emotional state that repeats itself every day creates real dysfunctions in our body.

Ninety per cent of the causes of human disease come from planes beyond the physical, and it is on these planes that symptoms begin to manifest before the physical body shows any disturbance. If we can identify the negative moods that crop up when we get sick, we can fight the disease better and heal faster. Using floral remedies you try to influence the deeper structures from which the disease originates. Bach flowers rebalance the emotions. They address only and exclusively how we react emotionally to the vicissitudes, experiences and problems in our days. They give great serenity and peace, courage or strength, they help us feel at the fullest of our possibilities.

They can be useful in the face of an illness, not from a physical point of view but just as a mood support. The person is seen as a complete individual where emotions are a pivotal point, and not just as a physical body with symptoms. It is therefore necessary to analyze the emotional state and not the physical symptoms, based on this the suitable remedies are found. In fact subjects with identical physical problems react and live with different emotions and feelings. Bach flowers have no contraindications and do not interact with medicines.

Bach has thus divided the 38 flowers from which the remedies are drawn. The very first flowers discovered by Bach were the so-called "12 Healers", which the Welsh doctor promptly began to experiment first on himself and then on his patients; the other 26 were discovered a short time later, divided into "7 Helpers" and "19 Assistants".

Dr Bach later abandoned the distinction between 'Healers', 'Helpers' and 'Assistants' as superfluous, but many people around the world still use it. Bach Flowers do not help to repress negative attitudes, but transform them into their positive side. The Bach Flowers associated with the first chakra are only in general, because the flowers must still be chosen based on the emotion that is not in harmony and must be balanced.

Water violet

It belongs to the category of "Healers" and was the tenth to be discovered by Dr. Edward Bach.

Who needs this flower is a person who has a lot of self-esteem, above the norm. She tends to be silent, calm, she never lets herself be influenced by the opinion of others, she often remains aloof, mysterious, dark, very reserved, haughty, willingly listens to other people's problems by giving advice. The problem with those with this nature is pride, she hardly apologizes and if wrong she has the ability to turn the situation around because she is convinced she is never wrong. However, we are responsible people who are appreciated and sought after by others, even if they are a little detached. "Home sweet home" is the motto of Water Violet. You feel safe in your environment, without too many jolts. This detachment from others can make you haughty or proud. Often their detachment is due to situations in which they could not express their emotional side. For this they close and stiffen.

The remedy can help bring them back into balance so that they can become more involved with others. Water Violets often suffer from eating disorders, hypertension, stomach aches, headaches. These characters are unable to express their feelings despite being their primary necessity; as a result, a small confrontation with Agrimony can be seen, he also hides his problems and is reluctant to express his true feelings, but for other reasons. In children, these characters are found in cases where they do not want to play and mix with others for pride. With Water Violet you are wise and go through life with kindness and discretion.

Moods and symptoms related to Water Violet in order of importance:

- Pride and confidentiality
- Confidentiality and independence
- You want to solve problems yourself
- Stiff neck
- Individuality
- Joint stiffness
- There is little talk

- **Definition of E. Bach**

For those who, in sickness or in health, like to be alone. Very quiet people, who move without making noise, speak little and in a low voice. Very independent, capable and confident. They do not attach great importance to the opinions of others. They are secretive, leave people alone and go their own ways. Often sharp and talented. The calm and tranquility that distinguish them are a blessing to those around them.

Impatiens

It belongs to the category of "Healers" and was the second plant discovered by Dr. Edward Bach.

Who needs this flower is an impatient person, speaks quickly, eats quickly, dresses quickly, combs quickly, makes up quickly, works quickly, walks quickly, thinks something and immediately acts. Everything is done in a hurry, moving from one thing to another. Slow people are not tolerated, so much so that one prefers to be alone at one's own pace, rather than following the times of others. Impatiens people need to learn that speed does not equal frenzy.

Another symptom of Impatiens is the intractability upon waking. With Impatiens you live your own pace and that of others with patience and availability. Impatiens concentrate is indicated for those who are easily irritable. Due to the impatience felt, the person thinks he has to do everything right away, and for this he adopts a high speed in his actions, thoughts and even in his way of speaking. Her competence and efficiency lead her to allow herself to be irritated and frustrated by slower colleagues and consequently to prefer to work alone. Due to her strong sense of independence she hates wasting time and in conversations often finishes the sentences of others for them.

They are always anxious characters and are subject to tachycardia, have digestive spasms, psycho-emotional disorders, neck pain, cramps and acidity.

It is also noted that this flower also works in hyperkinetic children, giving them calm and relief.

- The floral remedy is prepared with the solar method using by skipping the lilac-pink flowers, without touching them with the hands, and covering the surface of the water in the basin.

Impatiens-related moods and symptoms in order of importance:

- Advice and interference cannot be tolerated
- Impatience
- Idealism and impatience
- Hyperactivity for which you are constantly moving
- Annoyance for mishaps
- Stuttering from haste
- Bulimia with exaggerated hunger for which one can become aggressive
- Aggression due to impatience
- Hasty decisions
- Neck tense
- Accidents due to excessive haste
- Torticollis

- **Definition of E. Bach**

Those who are quick in thought and action and want everything done without hesitation or delay. When sick they anxiously desire a speedy recovery. They find it difficult to be patient with slow people, considering it a fault and a waste of time, and they go to great lengths to make such people more attentive. Often they prefer to work and think for themselves, to be able to do everything at their own pace.

Heater

It belongs to the "Aid" category.

Who needs this flower is a person who always tries to communicate with others even for small things, going in constant search of affection and consolation and it is only in this way that he draws his happiness; but if the contact is broken, for whatever reason, the suffering becomes torture. The problem is that she is afraid of being alone, so the need for company and to be heard becomes an obsession.

Heather needs love, to feel valued. In certain situations of suffering or faced with problems that arise, there is a great need to talk about it with others, but when this need to always have someone close becomes excessive and one cannot be alone, Heather comes to help by concentrating own energies within themselves and also making the relationship with others easier.

The person with this nature will never like solitude, she will gladly approach others to exchange a few words but this time she will interrupt the conversation with a positive attitude towards herself. She will always seek attention in the group but without going overboard and without complaining. Precious flower for those who feel self-centered and hypochondriac, who want to listen more to others, who have so much self-confidence and who feel competent that they never doubt their ability to advise or give support.

With Heather you are able to listen and connect with others. You find values for your life.

- To prepare the floral remedy, take the ears above the mature flowers, from several plants, and place them as quickly as possible on the water (sun method).

Heather-related moods and symptoms in order of importance:

- Talkative with anyone
- Need for constant attention
- To get attention we invent diseases
- Loneliness that is always avoided
- Easy crying
- Food as an obsession
- Possessiveness towards anyone for fear of loneliness
- Self-pity to get attention
- We talk a lot
- Self pity
- Food obsession
- Bulimia with talkativeness
- Anxiety due to excitement

- **Definition of E. Bach**

Those who are always looking for the company of anyone who is willing, finding it necessary to discuss their business with others, no matter who it is.

They are very unhappy if they have to be alone for any
time, be it short or long.

Chicory

It belongs to the category of "Healers" and is the fifth medicinal plant discovered by Edward Bach.

Whoever needs this flower is a person who dedicates his mental and physical strength to the needs of the people he loves, exercising a certain amount of control. Usually the person with this nature is easily recognized because he always has something to fix for the loved one: such as the collar of the shirt, the hair, the make-up, he also gives advice on clothing, on the partner, on friendships, and asks that it be reciprocated , as if it were a job, an assembly line I give to you, you give to me. You love others, but you want to be reciprocated. Classic interested manipulator character who probably won't easily accept this definition. But if it often comes to mind: after everything I've done, he looks at how he treats me. Then it's time to consider Chicory. The person with this nature will always think how to improve the life of the people he loves, because he wants them to be happy, but the flower remedy will help them understand that everyone has their own destiny to follow and that it is not necessary to manipulate; furthermore he will learn to give love, without expecting anything in return. With Chicory you understand the true qualities of love by giving protection and security to others in complete autonomy. It is prepared with the sun method, and since the flower withers quickly you need to have a basin with water ready.

Chicory related moods and symptoms in order of importance:

- Pride in your home
- Jealousy and possessiveness with those you love
- Jealousy with possessiveness
- Easy crying
- Exaggerated love for the house
- Hypochondriasis to get attention
- Critical meddling in other people's affairs
- Sense of abandonment in parents when their children become Depressed from not being loved
- Need for recognition
- Greed as greed
- Desire to command with authoritarianism
- Abandonment, for parents who recriminate when their children go their own way
- Need for order in model housewives
- Love as possessiveness towards others.

- **Definition of E. Bach**

Those who are attentive to the needs of others. They have a tendency to take excessive care of children, relatives, friends and always find something wrong to fix. They continue to fix what they think is wrong, and they take pleasure in doing so. They would always like to have those they love close by.

Agrimony

It belongs to the category of "Healers" and is the fourth medicinal plant that Edward Bach discovered in 1930.

Agrimony is for all those who are afraid to show their feelings, always smiling, often wear the mask of cheerful people, even when they suffer. They use stimulants when they have problems nagging them. In Agrimony the tension, internal anxiety is not manifested with others. What worries is kept hidden and masked with the desire to laugh at all costs. Sometimes Agrimony-type people use alcohol or stimulants to try to maintain this facade of serenity. They usually dislike loneliness, finding it more difficult to wear this mask when alone with themselves.

On the contrary, they always try to surround themselves with friends, parties and blinding lights, while at night, when they find themselves alone with their thoughts, that mental torture that they had managed to repress so well inexorably comes back to haunt them.

The Agrimony remedy helps people who have such a character trait to accept the darker sides of life and of their personality and come to terms with them, so that they become more complete human beings, without losing their sense of humour, but being able to laugh at one's problems to solve them rather than hide them. To prepare the floral remedy, the flowers that have just opened or in bud are picked, before bees or other insects have visited them, and are prepared with the sun method between June and August.

Moods and symptoms related to Agrimony in order of importance:

- Forced cheerfulness
- Anxiety hidden by cheerfulness
- Anxiety and fear
- Anxiety for which you eat even at night
- Tendency to avoid discussions
- Anxiety localized in the chest
- Nervous hunger
- Hidden inner conflicts
- Fear of discussions
- Tightness in the chest
- They bite their nails
- Teeth grinding in sleep

- **Definition of E. Bach**

Jovial, cheerful people, full of good humor who love tranquility and are disturbed by quarrels or contrasts, in order to avoid which they are willing to make great sacrifices. Though generally trouble-ridden, restless and preoccupied in body and spirit, they hide such grievances behind their good humor and pranksterism, and are considered good friends to know.

They often make excessive use of alcohol or drugs, to stimulate and help themselves to carry their crosses lightly.

Walnut

It belongs to the category of "Assistants".

Whoever needs this flower is in a life-changing situation or is in a condition in which they do not have the strength to change, such as: marriage, divorce, new job, climate change, retirement, menopause, bereavement, pregnancy, vacation, new partner. Taking Walnut when experiencing a change facilitates adaptation by discovering new resources to easily experience the new situation. It is also useful for those who are sensitive to the tensions of their surroundings and who tend to make them their own.

Also indicated for those suffering from meteoropathy (symptoms related to meteorological factors).

Walnut helps break ties with the past, thus allowing you to continue on your path with confidence and without excessive suffering. With Walnut you are protected in changes, you feel safe and each new phase is lived with ease. In paediatrics, Walnut is indicated when children are experiencing a very specific phase of maturation or growth, as in the case of a child who has fixed teeth erupting and removes the milk ones, or it is used in puberty and adolescence to facilitate body change.

Walnut-related moods and symptoms in order of importance:

- To facilitate any kind of change
- Menopause
- Hypersensitive to changes

- Stages of change
- Puberty
- Influencing
- Teething
- Inconstancy

- **Definition of E. Bach**

For those who have well-defined ideals and life ambitions that they are fulfilling, yet on rare occasions are tempted by the enthusiasm of others, convictions or strong opinions, to stray from their own ideas, goals, or work. The remedy gives constancy and offers protection from external influences.

Rescue Remedy

By combining two or more flowers together, personalized blends can be obtained, i.e. aimed at a particular and subjective need. However, there is a combination prepared by Bach himself for general use; it is the emergency remedy called Rescue Remedy, a mixture of five flowers, which according to Bach would be useful in more acute situations: extreme stress, panic attacks, fainting, bad news, but also physical traumas. We can consider this "elixir" as the 39th flower, in reality it is a combination of 5 flowers that Dr. Edward Bach developed it in 1934, starting to use it as a means of therapeutic first aid in all emergency conditions, from physical trauma (for example a headache) to psychic one, and also from mourning, abandonment, loss , to the exams to be taken, to the postpartum. There are immediate benefits such as calm, serenity, relief, security, rebalancing of inner energies in stressful or particularly challenging situations. It also helps reduce fear and nervousness. As well as by mouth, this remedy can also be applied to the temples or wrists, or directly to the painful area.
It consists of a blend of:

- Star of Bethlehem, against sudden shock. As the acid that contains its flower, if touched, makes you cry, so the remedy helps to release a repressed emotion or any kind of trauma. It helps those who feel pain for a pain that comes suddenly (bad news, job loss, illness, bereavement, accident) or for the inconsolable loss of loved ones.

- Rock Rose, against panic or terror. Its characteristic thorns mean that if a person comes into contact with the plant, they are paralyzed by pain, especially if they injure their legs, which prevents them from walking. In the same way, the flower is used for paralyzing panic attacks, for external and internal trembling, sweating, tachycardia and blocking of the ability to react in an emergency situation. The flower helps those who let themselves be overwhelmed by their emotions, when fear turns into extreme panic and one gets stuck, with shortness of breath and heart in the throat, unable to react. In Rescue Remedy it is used for maximum anguish, to deal with a strong and acute state of terror or fear triggered by a traumatic event, accident or sudden illness.

- Impatiens, to restore calm. It is a plant that greedily absorbs water from the ground until the excess exudes from the leaves. As an indication of its constant activity, throughout the summer it bears shoots, flowers and seeds at the same time, without following the rhythms of the other plants. Its action in the Rescue Remedy serves to moderate impatience, anxiety from anticipation, excessive impetus, agitation, frustration or irritability towards a situation, which imposes a waiting time.

- Clematis, against the tendency to sag, the feeling of pulling away just before passing out. This climbing plant cannot take root in the ground because it has a very small root. Its guides hang down and give it a floating appearance. Likewise, it serves people who can't keep their feet on the ground, whose mind slips away from the present to fantasize about the future or alternative versions of the present. In Rescue Remedy it helps above all to avoid fainting and to alleviate that state of confusion and daze that can appear in emergency situations, when one would like to escape from reality.

- Cherry Plum, against the fear of losing control, of going crazy. Apparently calm, the plant is internally processing the flowers that will be born prematurely and in a compulsive way. The flower is for those who are afraid of going crazy, of acting irrationally, of making extreme and rash gestures, even self-harming, giving vent to dangerous impulses. He can't stop the sense of screeching noise of a thousand terrible thoughts that crowd into his head in a real mental overwork. He has the urge to commit violent acts that he is horrified by. In Rescue Remedy it helps to regain calm, self-control and the ability to manage anger and all emotional states that can lead to violence.

It is the only remedy which, as a rule, is not prepared exclusively in liquid form, but also in lactose tablets and ointments. In the latter formulation, called "Rescue Cream" Crab Apple is added, the purification remedy, for its purifying effect; it can be useful on various occasions: traumas, small skin rashes, muscle pain and tension, dehydrated skin.

It is very useful, for example, in children, for small sudden fears, in cases of accidents, when receiving bad news (mourning, illness), sudden moments of anxiety, fears, panic attacks. Put 4 drops of Rescue Remedy in a glass of water and sip it; initially with small sips close together (even every two or three minutes), then as the symptoms subside, the number of intakes is reduced. If you don't have the availability or don't have the time to take a glass of water, you can take 4 drops of the pure remedy. The Rescue is an emergency remedy, and should be used as such. It cannot replace the daily use of Bach flowers. To obtain good results and to be in good health with flower therapy, it is important to hire the most suitable flowers for each one, personalizing them on the basis of the current situation.

Number of the seventh chakra

The number 1 is the seventh chakra number.
One is the first number used for counting and, therefore, is recognized as having great power; without it there would be no number system as we know it. Every number system we can imagine has its starting point. It is often seen as the origin of all things and represents perfection, the absolute and divinity in monotheistic religions.

- A person characterized by the One is a born leader, one who is predisposed to organize, to decide; a precise, independent, inventive and ingenious person.

Symbol of the Beginning, the One is par excellence the number from which an idea flourishes and represents the strength in pursuing enterprising personal initiatives. This characteristic leads the individual to face and overcome the obstacles scattered along his path with determination and courage. A person characterized by the One identifies very much with himself. When she is immature she tends to move without regard for others and the environment, while when she is more evolved she becomes a pioneer who points the way to her contemporaries by winning her own battles. The consequence of this will be a high predisposition to experiment, to make mistakes and to retrace one's steps, due to the constant and strenuous search for perfectibility. If he loses his freedom he becomes authoritarian, domineering, perfectionist, heavy-handed, pedantic with an excessive sense of duty. He is successful as a writer, director, president, public figure, business executive, designer. Affinity with other numbers:

- Fair: 4 and 7.
- Excellent: 2 and 6.

We can associate each number with a planet, a zodiac sign and a fundamental element of life on Earth. For Number 1 we have:

- Sign : Aries.
- Planet : Mars.
- Element : Fire.

Like the planet it associates with, this number gives great energy, aggression and spirituality which must be channeled well. It makes you eager to impose yourself and express your own way of being. Number ones show strong individuality and enjoy a lot of luck in every aspect of life. Ambition leads them to reach high positions. Qualities to be developed are tolerance and renunciation.

Color of number 1: Red.

- Laziness wins.
- Promotes blood circulation.
- Increases internal body heat.
- Fight apathy.
- Effective against colds.

- Fights melancholy and depression, useful in times when energy is lacking or when one feels exhausted.
- Conquers the first symptoms of a cold.
- Not recommended in cases of fever, hypertension, wounds, heartburn and inflammation.
- Stones: ruby, red jasper, garnet.

The archetype of number 1 is the Warrior.
His Shadow Number is the Rebel.
The Rebel, representing the shadow side of the Warrior, distinguishes strong and determined individuals, who, however, in their identification with the Archetype, oscillate between the opposing tendencies of courage and self-denial, doubt and insecurity.

- **The challenge**

Recognize your own worth with balance.
The Rebel has the same characteristics as the Warrior but undermined by insecurity and lack of self-esteem.
He yearns for recognition of his value by his neighbor, perhaps due to a lack of recognition by his father, a significant figure for the warrior whose symbols are the Sun and precisely the father. Example, a typical attitude of the rebel could be to have had an idea, but this is criticized or questioned.

- The Warrior examines these opposing options carefully and, if he deems them groundless, explains his reasons and continues to carry out his project, sure of his abilities.

- The Rebel, on the other hand, cannot bear that the thought of him is opposed, he opposes it, perhaps vehemently and then lets it all go, abandoning the project. Later reviewing his attitude and considering it a lack of him, he feels even more distrustful going to further undermine his self-esteem.

He may also fail to operate this retrospective, aggravating the situation with suspicions of manipulation by others; it is precisely the difficulty of accepting one's mistakes that is the challenge that the One should face. Lack of introspection can block his experimentation and the fear of failure can stop subsequent actions. The remedy for recognizing the shadow is the "here and now", being present to oneself gives the ability to review the scene and recognize where one went wrong in order to remedy it. Constancy and perseverance are needed, but by cultivating this attitude the person will be present when the event occurs and will be able to recognize the rebel before he acts and causes trouble.

Phisical exercises

- **Exercise 1**

Do some relaxation exercises by shaking your arms and legs.
Sit on the floor with your back straight and then do alternate breathing for a few minutes.

- **Exercise 2**

Assume the quadruped position and perform the "horse's back / cat's arched back" exercise 7 times.

- **Exercise 3**

Starting in a cross-legged position, close your eyes and extend your arms straight up with palms touching above your head.
The fingers are also pointing up and the spine should feel slightly tense.
Breathe deeply a few times from this position, then relax again, but trying to maintain the position for a few minutes over time.

- **Exercise 4**

Sit upright, place your ring fingers against each other and interlace the other fingers with the right thumb under the left.
Keep your hands at stomach height, close your eyes, inhale deeply through your nose and make a long "oooooomm" sound as you exhale.
Repeat the exercise 7 times focusing on the seventh chakra.

- **Exercise 5**

Lie on your back with your eyes closed and your muscles relaxed. The palm of the left hand touches the crown of the head, and the right is on top of the left.
Inhale and exhale completely relaxed.
Breathe deeper and deeper and imagine that you are receiving the energy of the universe through your crown chakra.
As you exhale, visualize energy flowing through your body, a white or golden light healing you.
Slowly place your hands on the ground along the body after a few minutes and stay relaxed a little longer..

Stones for the 7th Chakra

In crystallotherapy stones of the 7th Chakra are considered those of white or transparent color, of any type of brightness or transparency.

- The placement area of the stones is the top of the head, at the height of the fontanel.

The crystals that can rebalance the seventh chakra are: rock crystal (or hyaline quartz), diamond, rainbow obsidian, spinel, celestine, white onyx, moonstone, rutilated quartz, selenite, danburite.

- The most representative basic frequency stone is hyaline quartz, or rock crystal.
- The most representative advanced frequency stone is Danbyrite.

The transparent and white crystals are neutral minerals that simply convey the light towards us, reinforcing what is already present in us. They enhance the effect of other minerals. White stimulates purity and clarity.
The range of action of white minerals:

- Confer wealth at all levels.
- They give a sense of justice.
- They make you feel eternity.
- Confer purity.
- Give a feeling of peace.

Feel its energy passing through the sacral chakra as you hold it in your hand or wear it by ring or necklace. You don't have to buy them all, just choose the stones you prefer or which you already have.

Hyaline Quartz

The name of hyaline quartz derives from the Greek hyalos, which means glass, but it is also called with the name of rock crystal, which derives from the Greek word krustallos which means ice, due to the belief that rock crystal was formed from ice.

It is the most widespread mineral on earth and is formed in all environments and all types of rock, and has been known for a very long time.

Pliny the Elder mentions it in his Naturalis Historia, Homer in his Iliad describes its characteristics, Aztecs and Mayas used hyaline quartz skulls for power rituals, the ancient Greeks believed that the Gods drank Ambrosia, the famous nectar, from chalices of rock crystal, in Asia hyaline quartz has always been spoken of as "a stone of light detached from the celestial throne", while in Australian aboriginal mythology, quartz is the substance most commonly identified with the mystical substance called "mabain" with which the "wise men" (called karadjis) get their magical powers.

- Hyaline Quartz is the most versatile and powerful healing stone of all crystals, able to work on any condition. Remarkable is its ability to amplify the subtle energies around it, including those of all other crystals. It greatly strengthens the aura, and is used to activate and align all chakras, even the transpersonal chakras.

Rock crystal provides more energy, and stimulates the immune system to prevent serious diseases. It facilitates heart functioning, prevents heart attack, carries oxygen to the brain and stabilizes blood pressure. In meditation it strengthens one's energy field and when used together with hematite it facilitates grounding and rooting. It also allows for emotional clarity and purity of heart, amplifying spiritual insights. Generates electromagnetism and dissipates static electricity.

If hyaline quartz is combined with lepidolite, amber and tourmaline, it facilitates their functions.

Rainbow Obsidian

Obsidian is a volcanic glass that originates from the rapid cooling of silica-rich lava: the thermal shock prevents the formation of crystals and produces an amorphous and rigid mass, rich in inclusions of various minerals. Black in color and generally opaque, it can also take on a silver color (silver obsidian) if finely distributed gas bubbles are present in the original magma or a colorful and brilliant appearance if they are made of water (rainbow obsidian). If gray feldspars are found in the rock formation process then it takes on a white-grey speckled colouration, the so-called snowflake obsidian.

- It is the stone of the warrior, who faces everything with the calm and reflection of someone who is not afraid of death. Gives inner clarity, balance and harmony. Obsidian connects spirit and matter.

It facilitates introspection, brings the most hidden emotions and thoughts to the surface and allows the conscious mind to penetrate the dark sides of the personality, directing the individual towards the path of transformation. It purifies the ego because it works as a mirror, it destroys illusions and also reflects defects: it is the light that dissolves the dark, the self meets its shadow to understand and illuminate it. It is a stone of self-knowledge.

Obsidian also helps to release repressed emotions, inducing people who have excessive self-control to release censorship and act in harmony with their feelings. Like all black stones, obsidian moves stagnant and negative energies and disperses them, allowing to overcome the fears and traumas that block the individual's personal growth. It acts as a protective shield and seals the aura.

- Obsidian can be drained after use under running water. To obtain the best physical and spiritual effects, it is recommended to carry the stone in close contact with the skin, in the pocket or on painful areas, but never around the neck.

Warning

It should be used with caution by those with a strong emotional charge and better if accompanied by a rock crystal. With obsidian one becomes spiritually free and invulnerable "unsullied warriors". Thanks to this new wisdom, the latent faculties develop and one learns to see the truth better and better until one becomes clairvoyant.

Diamond

It is the hardest, most transparent and luminous stone that exists: pure carbon. It forms at a pressure of 40,000 atmospheres and at a temperature of over 2,000 degrees Celsius. It symbolizes purity, courage, strength, loyalty, mental clarity, divine wisdom. The Greeks and the Latins called it Adamas - Adamantis "the indomitable", "very hard iron", "steel", "unbreakable", since neither iron nor fire can damage this gem which can only be worked with other diamonds (it is insoluble to acids and unmistakable). Strengthens and purifies the body, removes blockages and negativity, awakens the Vital Energy and strengthens the aura, balances the hemispheres of the brain and has rebalancing virtues in general, eliminates toxins from the body. Tones the heart, increases physical endurance, stimulates awareness, increases will and control capabilities. It is indicated against fears and depression and in the treatment of disorders of the brain, nervous system and sensory system.

Its energy is powerful but must be used carefully and "one-time", as it has the ability to enhance both conscious positive characteristics and uncontrolled negative characteristics, such as rigidity, stubbornness, stubbornness of people who have not raised themselves sufficiently on a spiritual level (in very simple terms, such as "a Ferrari in the hands of a child"), then making the user unpleasantly aware, in a "drastic" way, of their own evolutionary stage not up to the situation (not by chance it is also called the "Stone of the strong").

In fact, it appears that some diamonds of enormous carat and value, "famous", have had the attribute of bad luck by their owners (for example the blue "Hope" diamond).

Diamond can also be used to amplify or energize the effect of other crystals.

Moonstone

Moonstone has been used for centuries in a variety of cultures. Being a perfect expression of yin energy, i.e. the mysterious and placid energy of the moon, this stone is in turn the bearer of calm, peace and balance.
The serenity and tranquility that the mineral generates has a sensual and extraordinary effect, infusing creativity and optimism with its soft glow.
Anciently, but still today, moonstone is considered a sacred stone in India.
Associated with the moon, the stone was worn by the goddess Diana and in the East moonstone amulets were often hung on fruit trees to ensure fertile and abundant crops and in the Middle Ages, by alchemists, it was believed that if held in the mouth, the stone di luna could help make appropriate decisions. Moonstone is a gem of intuition and deep understanding, it helps balance the emotional body by accentuating freedom of expression and particularly attenuates aggressive tendencies. By bringing feminine energy, moonstone opens up our more yin side, can stimulate pineal gland functioning, balance internal hormonal cycles with the rhythms of nature, relieve menstrual and pregnancy pain, promote fertility and help stimulate the lymphatic and immune system. It can reduce swelling and excess body fluid.
Although often considered a women's stone, moonstone can be very helpful to men in opening up their

emotional self. The finest moonstone is mainly mined from Sri Lanka. It helps to be more aware that all things are part of a cycle of constant change. The ideal and most resonant time to use moonstone is during the full moon phase. Thanks to its association with water, it appears to be very protective of people who live near seaside places. Moonstone connects the second and sixth chakras beautifully to each other, enhancing intuitive sensitivity through behaviors that are less overwhelmed by personal feelings. Works wonders when paired with garnet, (revealing the truth behind our illusions) and when used in conjunction with amethyst in the higher chakras.

- Moonstone is a very personal gem: it reflects the soul of the person who owns it. It does not take away or add anything to the personality, but shows it as it really is: this is why it is useful during meditation.

It is excellent for women, but can be indicated to men to encourage them to express their emotions. The gem is therefore used to stimulate the functioning of the pineal gland and the balance of internal hormonal cycles, adapting them to the rhythms of nature

In feng shui, moonstone is used for its calming properties, its yin energy and the fact that it recalls the element of water. A home or office with too much yang energy can benefit from the compensation that the stone will be able to generate. Make sure you take the best care of your moonstone, whether it's spheres and ovals, or jewelry. Clean it often and gently, trying to preserve it from exposure to strong sunlight.

As you can easily guess, unlike other crystals and other stones, the best way to recharge the stone is by exposing it to moonlight. You can choose the fresh energy of the new moon or the powerful vibrations of the full one: by taking care of your gem, you will receive abundance, energy and balance in return.

White onyx

The white onyx stone was very popular with the ancient Greeks, Romans and Egyptians. Its name comes from the Greek word "onux", which means "nail". Legend has it that one day Cupid cut the divine nails of Venus with an arrowhead while she was sleeping and the Fates (the three daughters of Zeus who wove the thread of every man's destiny) immediately changed them into stone, so that no part of the divine body of Venus could ever be destroyed. The ancient Egyptians believed that white onyx could cool sexual ardor when overdone.

The properties of white onyx keep the memory of physical events surrounding a person. A strong stone to be used for psychic work as it tells the story of the wearer. A stone of strength, good for sportsmen or people under mental and emotional stress. The white onyx stone brings balance to the mind and body, and is a wonderful stone for those who are fickle by nature, as it helps to keep us grounded and focus our attention. Traditionally it can be particularly useful for skin diseases, healing infected wounds, fungal infections, inflammation and even sunburn. It helps to predict what lies beyond and to become the master of one's future, removing unnecessary dependencies on the growth process, especially unhealthy or annoying emotional and emotional involvements.

Rutilated Quartz

Rutilated quartz is a type of quartz that contains rutile (titanium dioxide) in needle form. Rutile needles can be reddish, or they can be golden, silver, or on very rare occasions, greenish in color.

The inclusions of rutilated quartz have been called Venus hair since the Middle Ages, and from that period the belief that the stone can slow down the aging process was born. Rutilated quartz is a stone that has both the energetic vibration energy of clear quartz and the amplifying power of rutile, which makes it very useful when combined with other stones, especially labradorite, citrine and chalcopyrite . The properties of rutilated quartz make it an illuminator for the soul, a stone to promote spiritual growth.

- The stone is known to be an energizing stone that helps in gaining and releasing energy on all levels. It is also said to relieve imposed loneliness and ease the guilt feelings generated by others, thus making happiness possible.

It can increase one's autonomy and self-esteem by instilling the ability to find one's own path. It is a useful stone for eating disorders, and the absorption of nutrients from food, tissue regeneration, fatigue, and depression.

It is used for meditation, spiritual communications, and lucid dream work.

Stone particularly suitable for the search for greater spiritual experiences and meditation on feminine energies.

Rutilated quartz can be useful for moving energy along the meridians and in physical areas where energy stagnates.

Selenite

Selenite owes its term to the Greek "selenites" literally "moonstone", from the name of the Greek goddess of the moon, Selene. Not to be confused with moonstone, another of the most beautiful and luminescent gemstones.

Selenite contains a lot of feminine energy and is often used to connect and communicate with the Divine. In the past it was often used as a magic wand to facilitate the conveyance of one's intentions for the Higher Self or the Universe.

Selenite is the stone of tranquility, it gives a very high vibration, and is capable of instilling mental clarity and a deep sense of inner peace, providing flexibility to our nature and strength for our important decisions.

It is a stone that goes well with intense spiritual work, especially in meditation, as well as being a powerful crystal of psychic communication. It can aid in communication in the past tense with ancestors and spirit guides.

Selenite also has the wonderful property of being able to energetically purify and cleanse other crystals of heavy energies. It can help at the cellular level, the spine and the skeletal system, it is used to improve skin tone and the body's ability to absorb calcium. Ancient popular beliefs, but common all over our planet, have also emphasized the use of selenite to increase libido. The properties of selenite are often used in magic to evoke protection from the realm of the dead and to also dispel negative energy in environments.

Excellent reveals itself in esotericism if used on special grids, or around the house or in the corners of a room (together with the salt, but without touching each other), to create a safe and peaceful space.

Celestine

Celestine, from the Latin "caelestis" which means "celestial", was so named for its very ethereal appearance. Celestina is a stone of peace and harmony which induces a vision of real peaceful coexistence with the entire universe.

Also called "heaven stone" due to its soft celestial color, it was believed to have been created by choirs of Heavenly Angels. In New Age circles celestine is said to be native to the stars known as the Pleiades (commonly called the "Seven Sisters") and that the stone holds celestial wisdom. Balances Yin and Yang energies, the two polarities of the body. Transform anger and fury constructively, helping to overcome limitations. Harmonizes the mind to high frequencies, improves intellectual abilities.

Celestine has a very high frequency and is a very spiritual stone that can help open portals to one's Higher Self. Known for expanding creativity it is often used in the arts.

Accelerates spiritual development and brings a general sense of peace.

www.ingramcontent.com/pod-product-compliance
Lightning Source LLC
LaVergne TN
LVHW050614200726
843508LV00010B/1847